Cosmic Grooves:

Leo

Y0-BBE-101

Cosmic Grooves:

Leo

by Jane Hodges

CHRONICLE BOOKS
SAN FRANCISCO

RHINO

Text copyright © 2001 Chronicle Books LLC
Executive Producer: Andrea Kinloch
Compilation Produced for Release: Dave Kapp, Mark Pinkus, and Andrea Kinloch
Remastering: Bob Fisher at Pacific Multimedia Corp.
Licensing: Wendi Cartwright
Project Assistance: Patrick Milligan, Amy Utstein, Mary Patton, and Mason Williams

Rhino Entertainment Company
10635 Santa Monica Blvd.
Los Angeles, California 90025
www.rhino.com

All rights reserved. No part of this book may be reproduced in any form
without written permission from the publisher.
Page 48 constitutes a continuation of the copyright page.

Library of Congress Cataloging-in-Publication Data available.

ISBN 0-8118-3065-9

Printed in China

Designed by Michael Mabry
Illustration copyright © 2001 Michael Mabry

Distributed in Canada by Raincoast Books
9050 Shaughnessy Street
Vancouver, British Columbia V6P 6E5

10 9 8 7 6 5 4 3 2 1

Chronicle Books LLC
85 Second Street
San Francisco, California 94105
www.chroniclebooks.com

TABLE of CONTENTS

- 6 Leo
- 8 Introducing Leo
- 10 Dedicated to Leo
- 12 Leo at Work
- 13 Leo Careers
- 14 Leo in Love
- 15 Leo Relationships
- 16 Miss Leo and Her Men
- 29 Mr. Leo and His Women
- 42 Leo at Home
- 43 Leo Health
- 44 Leo Style
- 45 On the Road with Leo
- 46 Leo Entertaining
- 47 In the Company of Leo

Leo

July 23 to August 23

Element: *Fire*
Quality: *Fixed, a sign that provides consistency*
Motto: *"I create"*
Planetary Ruler: ☉ *The Sun, the planet of warmth and self-expression*
Sun's Influence: *Extroverted Leos radiate warmth and creativity without even trying. These fiery folks want to share their passions with the world—and have the world applaud. When properly channeled, Leo energy creates excitement and sets social trends. Misused, this sign's quest for self-expression becomes a shallow or dictatorial quest for attention.*
Symbol: *Lion*
Lion's Influence: *Like lions, folks born under this sign roar loudly and often. They skip subtlety and make grand entrances, demand adoration, and relish life in the limelight. They love luxury and aren't afraid of coming off as vain—in fact, they want everyone to know that only the best is good enough for them. They encourage others to play and indulge in life's pleasures. These big-hearted folks love parties and drama, and wear their hearts on their sleeves. For both the male and female Lion, life's a big celebration where they preside and their loved ones are the guests of honor.*

How to recognize a Leo:
Full head of hair, outrageous clothing, flirtatious eye contact
Pick-up line: *"What have you already heard about me?"*
What a Leo wants:
Adoration, power
What a Leo needs:
Love, creative outlet
Jukebox selection: *"Everybody Wants to Rule the World"*

Introducing Leo

Leos are the zodiac's superstars and lovers. Ruled by the fiery and life-giving sun ☉, Leos create heat and drama wherever they go. Those born under this sign have a deep need to express themselves and create an impact on their immediate environment. They take great pains to choose highly prestigious or outrageous clothing, hairstyles, makeup, and even vocabulary that set them apart from others—then they watch and await the royal reception. Leos want others to worship them, or at least admire them. To get attention, they give attention and lavish loved ones with praise, encouragement, and high expectations. They are anything but subtle in their quest to like the good life—and look good doing it.

Charming Leo kids know just how to attract an audience. Affectionate and extroverted, they show a talent for drama (and tantrums) at an early age. Lion kids love to play dress-up and put on shows. Leo teens appease their need to belong by either adhering closely to a clique—a tactic that, ironically, reinforces their insecurity—or by diving into creative activities like theater that give them the limelight in a more constructive way. Leos love to date and play the field; but when they've found someone they really care for, they require a strong commitment. Leo youths almost always choose a well-known celebrity or political figure as a role model, since they aspire to international fame or power. Leo adults love to have a good time and cultivate their innate sense of humor and drama. Lions are popular social and romantic companions, because they encourage others to enjoy themselves. They also like playing amateur therapist. In fact, sharing confidences with a Leo is the best way to compliment one.

Though they demand a lot of attention—and will create scenes to get good service from waiters, cab drivers, spouses, and kids—Lions are always straightforward about what they want. Life, to a Leo, is about self-expression and love. A Leo deserves only the best—and encourages others to think the same way. They shower their friends with humor and good times, and expect—and get—the same in return.

Dedicated to Leo

Lions need dramatic music to reflect their personalities. They seek songs to highlight their sweeping entrances or that motivate people to dance.

Charismatic	Lion folks want to be their own boss—and everyone else's, too. *Everybody Wants to Rule the World* by Tears for Fears makes an excellent mission statement for this sign.
Chivalrous	Leo men are both gallant and macho, and *I'm the Man* by Joe Jackson celebrates their pride as well as their penchant for chivalry.
Inspired	This sign loves to party and revel in drama. *Wonderful World, Beautiful People* by Jimmy Cliff reminds the world that extroverted Lions see life as a celebration.
Volatile	Lions are as fiery as they are spontaneous—and *Firecracker* by Mass Production warns the world that these traits apply to their unforgettable tempers, too.
Positive	In *Accentuate the Positive*, Dr. John celebrates Lions' ability to bring out the best in others and to see the upside in any challenging situation.
Popular	It's not easy leading the crowd, but *Leader of the Pack* sung by The Shangri-Las is the perfect description of the way Leos innately steal the spotlight.

Magnetic	Even in small doses, the bold Leo persona can go a long way, which is what *Leo Rising* by Ronnie Montrose reminds the world.
Enthusiastic	Leo folks rarely get up on the wrong side of the bed. Each day gives Lions something new to look forward to, which is exactly what The Rascals capture in *A Beautiful Morning*.
Shameless	Leos just can't hide their feelings—especially when they're happy—and *You Make Me Feel Like Dancing* by Leo Sayer celebrates this sign's passion for love.
Outspoken	Crossing an opinionated Leo is ill-advised, and *Drama Queen* performed by Belloluna describes the unforgettable response Lions will give if they sense a surprise attack.
Adored	Whether out on the town or at an intimate party, charismatic Lions always want to know that they have the most important spot on their lover's dance card. *Save the Last Dance for Me* by The Drifters aptly describes the position Leo seeks in any situation.
Proud	From humble and arrogant to loving and dramatic, the archetypes of the Leo personality are mythologized in *Leo* by Cannonball Adderley.

Leo at Work

Born under a fire sign, Leos are creative and inspired by their need to put their own unique stamp on any assignment. They need a career that lets them express themselves, pays enough to support their lavish lifestyle, and allows them to lead others. While Leos may seem melodramatic in their personal lives, they're very organized at work and have an inherent understanding of how the power structure in any organization operates. Bossy Leos need to lead, even if doing so isn't part of their job description. The Lion boss makes work a mission of utmost importance and makes it clear he or she will take it personally if staff members don't try hard. If successful, the Lion will take all due credit (and then some) for workers' success. Because Leos are susceptible to false flattery, they will need at least one trusted coworker who gives them honest feedback. They also like to carve out a domain of sorts around their work area, and they'll regale colleagues with funny stories and coffee talk so there's a regular following outside their cube.

Leo Careers

Leo workers need to feel that the show couldn't go on without them, so they often opt for creative jobs in the entertainment industry as performers or as film and television moguls. A Leo will infuse even a conservative job with a dramatic touch. A Leo who works in law will view the defense process as an opportunity to perform before the jury; a Leo publicist or teacher will try to entertain and surprise others rather than just arm them with facts. Lions Roman Polanski, Stanley Kubrick, and Ken Burns all built distinguished film careers—a Leo specialty. Company founders and CEOs, like Leos Samuel Goldwyn and Max Factor, exemplify the role that most Leos want. Even better than a job as CEO is a job where the Lion gets paid to be a "personality"—working as a sportscaster, spokesperson, or professional athlete appeals to this sign. Leos Connie Chung and Garrison Keillor had success respectively as TV and radio personalities. Since Leos love nothing better than having a good time, they have an innate knack for managing restaurants, clubs, or theaters and for event planning, where creating a good social environment is important.

Leo in Love

Leos love dating, and play the field for quite some time before settling into a relationship. These jealous folks need constant reassurance that they have a partner's full devotion. In return, Leos spoil their mates with fine dinners, compliments, surprises, and gifts. The right partner for the charismatic Lion is an upbeat, appreciative person who can ground an idealistic Leo in reality. While no Leonine romance would be complete without frequent fighting and tears, the makings-up will more than compensate for the conflicts. Once married, the Lion doesn't settle into routine. Those born under this sign want to see and be seen in all the best places, and having a life partner makes both male and female Lions all the more eager to show off the wonderful person they love. Any Leo mate needs to keep a pair of polished dancing shoes on hand.

Leo Relationships

Leo & Aries (*March 21 to April 20*)	Passionate
Leo & Taurus (*April 21 to May 21*)	Harmonious
Leo & Gemini (*May 22 to June 21*)	Passionate
Leo & Cancer (*June 22 to July 22*)	Challenging
Leo & Leo (*July 23 to August 23*)	Harmonious
Leo & Virgo (*August 24 to September 22*)	Challenging
Leo & Libra (*September 23 to October 23*)	Passionate
Leo & Scorpio (*October 24 to November 22*)	Harmonious
Leo & Sagittarius (*November 23 to December 21*)	Passionate
Leo & Capricorn (*December 22 to January 20*)	Harmonious
Leo & Aquarius (*January 21 to February 20*)	Passionate
Leo & Pisces (*February 21 to March 20*)	Challenging

Miss Leo and Her Men

Few men can keep their eyes off glamorous Leo ladies like Mae West, Halle Berry, and Myrna Loy. Even Leo women who play up their comic side—like Victoria Jackson and Lisa Kudrow—command attention for their silly antics and sex appeal.

Women born under this sign have plenty of dating options, a point they'll make clear to any man who approaches. Miss Leo's ideal partner will treat her to the very best and play a great audience during her dramas, but the relationship will develop only if he's strong enough to challenge her from time to time.

Leo Woman & Aries Man

Tori Amos seeks Marvin Gaye.

Miss Leo gets a kick out of this sporty, optimistic man. He doesn't spend his time worrying about how to impress other people—he just goes after what he wants. Both Miss Leo and Mr. Aries are blunt, occasionally tactless people. While their sharp comments often upset thin-skinned friends, they can communicate well with one another and appreciate, rather than resent, the candor they share. They may clash over who's the boss in this relationship, but Mr. Aries will not let this woman get away with her typical dramatics (except sometimes, when her tantrums turn him on). He can help her to stop worrying about appearances. While he likes excitement and attention as much as she does, he teaches her that life isn't a dress rehearsal and she need not worry about turning every head in every room she enters. In bed, their playful dynamic will satisfy—and exhaust—both of them. This relationship has great marriage potential.

Leo Woman & Taurus Man

Patti Austin seeks Roy Orbison.

This sexy, quiet man presents a challenge to Miss Leo. He's stubborn and set in his ways, but sensual and successful. He's aloof, macho, and doesn't fall for her attention-getting dramas. He won't respond to sass, but he will respond to her charisma. In fact, sexually, this is a very good relationship for both of them. There are other hurdles, however. Mr. Taurus likes routine, for instance, while Miss Leo likes variety. While they both want high-quality belongings and appreciate fine art, Mr. Taurus is a collector, while Miss Leo wants to attend show openings to name-drop. They may also clash over money. Taureans like to save for a rainy day, while Leos like to live for the moment and recoup losses through high-risk methods like stock market speculation or gambling. If they keep separate checking accounts, the harmony they create in the bedroom can extend to the rest of their relationship. Both are faithful to lovers, and willing to work to please their partners.

Leo Woman & Gemini Man

Aimee Mann seeks Morrissey.

She's sexy, witty, fun, and loves to flit from one social event to the next—just like Mr. Gemini—but sometimes this man just doesn't give Miss Leo the attention she deserves. She won't allow his halfway idea of commitment. She's used to men dropping everything for her, but she may actually find herself going out of her way to pursue Mr. Gemini. The tension is intoxicating—and makes for excellent bedroom scenes. Mr. Gemini can humble arrogant Miss Leo by reminding her she can't own him; Miss Leo can draw out distracted Mr. Gemini by teaching him to share his thoughts fully. This relationship will help them both develop and will never grow dull. Mr. Gemini's insistence on autonomy is a perfect foil for Miss Leo's insistence that her needs come first. He can learn to be a more giving lover, and she can learn to accommodate the sort of person she can't control—which, ironically, allows her to know love more fully.

Leo Woman & Cancer Man

Lucille Ball seeks Arlo Guthrie.

Lady Leo gets a kick out of quiet Mr. Cancer. She gets him to laugh, and it's easy to seduce this sentimental man. It's clear that he appreciates her creativity and will be there for her when she comes home from a long day of work. They both love fine dining, but while Miss Leo loves to be seen at the latest restaurants, Mr. Cancer will convince her they should cook gourmet and then curl up by the fireplace. These two needy people can provide one another with the reassurance they both desperately seek. They communicate well—there's no mistaking how Miss Leo feels at any given time—and while Mr. Cancer may be harder to read, he will make it clear he can't live without her. They love to be surrounded by friends and family, and Mr. Cancer doesn't mind if Miss Leo insists on being the center of attention. If his loved ones are near him, that's all the satisfaction he needs. They both want a family to coddle and protect, and will make sentimental, loving parents, not to mention loving, stable spouses.

Leo Woman & Leo Man

Madonna seeks Mick Jagger.

All the world's a stage in this relationship. When two Leos, both intent on developing their own persona, get involved with one another, they have to work extra-hard to develop their relationship. Mr. Leo and Miss Leo are both so self-centered that they're not sure how to handle falling in love with one another. This relationship is a difficult, but ultimately rewarding, exercise for both of them, especially in the king-sized bed that serves as a shrine to their legendary sex drives. They'll squabble over all sorts of little details, since they both prefer big-idea thinking. However, over time, they realize they'll never win these day-to-day battles with one another. These tiny arguments, though, serve as the way that they communicate their need for one another. It's not an easy relationship, but no relationship is easy when it's built on true passion and connection—the things Leos want most from a mate.

Leo Woman & Virgo Man

Ginger Spice seeks Harry Connick Jr.

She wants the best money can buy, and he wants to be the best he can possibly be. He's not very glamorous, so her first instinct is to look elsewhere for fun. As time passes, though, this quiet man demonstrates a kindness, consideration, and selflessness that she admires. In fact, he's the guy she always calls when she's having trouble with one of the macho men who come and go in her life. He listens patiently to her laments and does his best to help her recover from the drama she describes. He's too shy to seduce her, so she'll put the moves on him—and end up pleasantly surprised by this sensual lover, even if he doesn't go in for some of the kinkier acts she likes. This sweet man teaches her to make more objective decisions and consider others' feelings, while she can teach him to loosen up and live a little. She's touched by his shyness as much as he's impressed with her bravado. Mutual admiration keeps the fires burning here.

Leo Woman & Libra Man

Belinda Carlisle seeks Sting.

Romeo has landed. He's handsome, stylish, and popular—not to mention unabashedly romantic. Mr. Libra knows how to flatter women. He's a flirt and a politician, always polite and always trying to win approval. Miss Leo is a diva and a superstar, always trying to win others' attention—even if it comes in the form of raised eyebrows and gossip. He can accept her loud personality, flashy clothes, and over-the-top comments. Since he dislikes fights, he will quickly apologize or acknowledge her demands to prevent them—yet elicit a thank you from her for making the accommodation. Both of them are vain, so they enjoy shopping, traveling, and going through money quickly. Sexually, they hit it off—he loves to please women, and her expressiveness leaves no doubt that she enjoys being with him. She can get Mr. Libra to speak his mind more often, while he can soften this brassy lady's approach. They both flatter and spoil one another in private, and others wish to discover the happiness this duo has found in one another.

Leo Woman & Scorpio Man

Connie Stevens seeks Lyle Lovett.

This brooding man's quiet intensity makes her heart flutter. They both have a need to possess their partners and demand nothing but full devotion from a significant other. Mr. Scorpio understands her need for constant demonstrations of loyalty and that her tantrums manifest an emotion he, too, feels—the desire for true love. He's a jealous man, but his possessive nature doesn't offend Miss Leo; in fact, she likes it. The problem this pair must overcome involves Miss Leo's need for publicity, which conflicts with Mr. Scorpio's need for privacy. She wants to share their love with the world—the tears, the French kisses, the laughter—while he likes to protect the sacredness of their relationship by keeping emotional displays private. Sexually, there will be plenty of display between these two; they both know how to focus on what a lover wants and aren't afraid to provide it. If they can find a way for Miss Leo to get the drama she wants—and Mr. Scorpio to get the privacy he requires—they will have mastered the only hurdle this duo will encounter.

Leo Woman & Sagittarius Man

Maureen McGovern seeks Donnie Osmond.

He's just back from an unbelievable adventure, and she's ready to take him for another thrilling ride. This worldly man is always on the prowl for a new adventuring companion, so he willingly takes on this classy lady. Miss Leo has a hard time seeing beyond her immediate surroundings, but life with Mr. Sagittarius takes her to physical and spiritual places she's never been. He can handle her demands, and he's every bit as funny, spirited, and improvisational as she is. Generous Miss Leo accepts the fact that Mr. Sagittarius sees life as a journey and pats him on the back for taking risks. He's not as luxury-oriented as she is, but he knows how to provide the romance she needs. Their physical attraction remains strong over time, as does the friendship that serves as a foundation for their relationship.

Leo Woman & Capricorn Man

Juliana Hatfield seeks Rod Stewart.

She can see through his restrained demeanor to the lusty, driven man who needs a flamboyant Lion woman in his life. Both Miss Leo and Mr. Capricorn are ambitious and competitive, but they use different methods to work their way into the "in" crowd. Miss Leo plays the diva who won't take no for an answer, while Mr. Capricorn uses his polite manners and good breeding to quietly get what he wants. This makes them an excellent couple: Miss Leo lends this subtle man a dash of charisma, while he adds some class to her over-the-top approach. In private, he relishes her devilish bedroom manner, and Miss Leo enjoys his passionate side. While he may not always be as romantic as she'd like, Mr. Capricorn is a good provider who takes his mate seriously. He's going places in life—and she'll happily go with him.

Leo Woman & Aquarius Man

Whitney Houston seeks Bobby Brown.

Mr. Aquarius and Miss Leo are opposites who attract. She'll encourage this master of group consciousness to express himself individually, while he'll motivate her to get beyond her need for individual fame and be a better and more generous citizen. If she wants love and acceptance, righteous Mr. Aquarius thinks she should take his approach and connect to the people around her by listening to them more. Miss Leo will teach Mr. Aquarius that if he projects himself more (and accepts her wardrobe makeover), he'll be a better member of the groups he champions. In bed, her focus and his experimentation make for hours of pleasure. These two challenge each other, but in a healthy way. Their differences soften over time as their love for one another grows.

Leo Woman & Pisces Man

Kate Bush seeks Michael Bolton.

This spiritual, dreamy man knows how to provide the kind of romantic surprises Miss Leo needs, but doesn't quite have the drive to provide the lifestyle she wants. If she's the breadwinner here, however, the two of them can share a spiritual connection. While Miss Leo may inadvertently hurt his feelings with her blunt demands and forthright criticisms, Mr. Pisces understands that her need for drama is really just her cry for love. He can teach her to convert her passion for life into compassion for others, while she can teach the most unselfish man in the zodiac that now and then he should put himself first. His gentle affections in bed may clash with her more athletic approach to lovemaking, but both these signs like to please, so this duo will work out their differences in no time. He'll let Miss Leo boss him around, while she'll get this sensitive man to see the world her way. They make an odd couple, but if they remember to encourage each other they'll be two of the happiest oddballs around.

Mr. Leo and His Women

Arnold Schwarzenegger and Antonio Banderas display Leo's typical lord-of-the-jungle animal magnetism. More civilized Leo men, like David Duchovny and Kevin Spacey, display a smug and more reserved kind of charisma. These guys love to flatter—and receive flattery from—their mates. While looking for the perfect love, Mr. Leo seduces many women and breaks lots of hearts. Once committed, though, he resolves to protect, shelter, and spoil his mate.

Leo Man & Aries Woman

Tony Bennett seeks Aretha Franklin.

This outspoken woman isn't afraid to look Mr. Leo in the eye and tell him what she thinks. Fortunately for both of them, Miss Aries thinks he's great. He'll discover her candor has a downside, though—she won't think twice about calling out his vanity or ignoring his attempts to boss her around. These two sporty people love to compete. While she wants to be first, fastest, and smartest, he wants to be most admired, most popular, and most attractive. Together they encourage one another to participate in these self-defined battles. They also know just how to coax each other out of blue periods. Miss Aries reminds Mr. Leo that he need not worry so much about others' opinions—after all, she's his biggest fan. Mr. Leo reminds Miss Aries she need not race her way to success, as he'll stay at her side and help her get there in style. Sexually, this pair of firebrands knows how to make sparks. Their marriage will remain honest, fun-filled, and exciting.

Leo Man & Taurus Woman

Buddy Holly seeks Barbra Streisand.

This sensual lady offers the perfect ultra-feminine contrast to Mr. Leo's macho bravado. However, beneath her lovely, steady exterior rests one of the most stubborn minds he's ever encountered. The main thing these two seemingly easygoing people share is a headstrong nature. Mr. Leo makes himself the center of attention and the life of the party, which means he requires a lavish shopping and entertaining budget. Miss Taurus, on the other hand, prefers to preserve her material security by spending quiet evenings at home and pursuing savvy retirement investments. If they can recognize that they're both unnaturally preoccupied with routine desires—Mr. Leo with social acceptance, Miss Taurus with material security—they can work toward a compromise. Their opposing natures make for heated bedroom scenes, while their shared devotion to partnership—even in hard times—will help them strike a balance between indulgence and practicality.

Leo Man & Gemini Woman

Coolio seeks Lauryn Hill.

Miss Gemini is one of those rare women who don't drop everything for a man. In between her book group, busy career, and travel to foreign countries, she manages to juggle at least a dozen suitors. In fact, she has multiple phone lines to handle their in-coming calls. She's the only woman who ever puts Mr. Leo on hold—and gets away with it. The fact that she's hard to get, coupled with the fact she keeps showing up at Mr. Leo's favorite haunts on another man's arm, convinces this proud Lion that she's worth chasing. The game is exciting to both of them. He's that rare man who's actually persistent with her, and she loves his idea of a good time: quirky presents, romantic dinners, and weekend getaways. In bed, they both like to experiment and never tire of surprising one another. He can teach her that loving one person is a far richer experience than flirting with everyone. She'll teach him that if he wants something, he has to give up a little ego to get it. There's just enough mystery between them to keep them chasing one another for a lifetime.

Leo Man & Cancer Woman

LL Cool J seeks Li'l Kim.

This dainty woman needs a man to take care of her. When she cries at sad movies, he'll sit by her side with tissues. They're not subtle about the courtship—or about anything having to do with their feelings. Miss Cancer needs to feel that she has someone to nurture and support, someone with marriage potential. Mr. Leo feels he needs a woman he can put on a pedestal and worship, and adores this woman who always reassures him of her commitment to him—and only him. There will be some tears and harsh words from time to time; she is as thin-skinned as he is bristly. However, these two genuinely need one another and quickly come to feel that a life without a permanent commitment wouldn't be worth living. Sexually, they feel privileged to know each other's most intimate secrets and desires. It's a relief to them both when they officially declare their love. Miss Cancer wants her familiar partner nearby, while Mr. Leo wants to show the world how great she is. They'll spend so much time together that they'll be married long before he proposes.

Leo Man & Leo Woman

Chuck D seeks Jennifer Lopez.

When the zodiac's two most self-centered, romantically preoccupied characters decide they're falling in love, they begin to make some unusual discoveries about themselves. In the past, Miss Leo found men to worship her, and Mr. Leo found women to humor his ego while he plied them with presents and romantic dinners. When these two Lions each encounter the other's self-absorption, they can choose to walk away—or give up some of their own selfish habits. Giving up one's ego is the biggest act of love around. If they manage to accomplish this, they'll be better people together than they are when they're apart. Their bedroom scenes will be as dramatic as the sweeping entrances of this winning act—one that will last a lifetime.

Leo Man & Virgo Woman

Isaac Hayes seeks Chrissie Hynde.

Her faithfulness and conservatism blend well with his bravado and boisterous nature. She'll blush when he asks her out and begins to heap on the compliments. Flustered by his attention, she'll begin to tell him about ways he could improve and organize his life. At first, he'll take offense when she advises him to stop smoking cigars, cut down on red meat, and take his Jaguar in for emissions testing. Then Mr. Leo will realize that this sweet lady is trying to help him improve his enjoyment of life. In bed, Miss Virgo is shy, but he can teach her, over time, to loosen her inhibitions. He's proud to unearth this innocent-looking woman's sensual side. She's a good listener, and will let him know when he's making a mistake. She'll also let him know she loves him—and that she could spend a lifetime making his life great.

Leo Man & Libra Woman

Dan Fogelberg seeks Toni Braxton.

These two balance each other well. Where Mr. Leo is tactless, Miss Libra is all manners. Where Miss Libra is afraid to make a decision that might offend someone, Mr. Leo is all action. If she can guard against her tendency to let him take charge in every area of their lives, they can build an equal relationship. They're both susceptible to flattery and share a similar vanity and a social-climbing side. They both enjoy the romance of their relationship as much as its consummation in the bedroom. While Mr. Leo puts a great deal of care into the way he presents himself and his feelings, Miss Libra puts a lot of thought into what she says and tells him all the time how important he is to her. Because they love to get decked out in their best outfits, they can stun crowds together. Miss Libra loves being adored by macho Mr. Leo, and he's proud to have her at his side.

Leo Man & Scorpio Woman

Robert Cray seeks Rickie Lee Jones.

This ice queen makes Mr. Leo's heart flutter. Sexual sparks will fly between these two possessive, powerful characters. However, they will also play mind games with each other. Miss Scorpio is happy to let this man think he's in control—but in fact giving him the impression he's in charge is her way of controlling him. When Mr. Leo discovers her tactics, the struggle between them may intensify. What these two share is a passion for life's highs and lows, as well as a jealous streak. They each want a partner who provides constant companionship, but they have different ideas of what companionship means. Mr. Leo makes their private life public, while Miss Scorpio resists sharing their life with outsiders. If they can agree on boundaries between these two worlds, they can share an intense but ultimately gratifying relationship.

Leo Man & Sagittarius Woman

Robert Plant seeks Tina Turner.

Even if she's not as stylish as he is, and could care less about being popular, there's something seductive about her. Sporty Miss Sagittarius loves adventures and having a good time. She can teach Mr. Leo to let go of his need for an audience—to live in the moment—and instead meditate on life's deeper meanings. He may envy her genuine spontaneity, as he has to work hard to maintain his air of amusement and excitement. Miss Sagittarius never worries about material things, and doesn't wait to see if her good deeds will be returned. She takes what she needs from others, and gives back when she has more than enough. Miss Sagittarius is one of the few women who can get Mr. Leo to check his ego at the door and loosen up and have a good time. They'll be friends as well as lovers, and if they marry, neither will regret it.

Leo Man & Capricorn Woman

Jerry Garcia seeks Janis Joplin.

She's that rare woman who's as career-driven as he is. They share the same dreams: the big window office, the business card that says CEO, and the vacation home in a world-class spot. They're both willing to suffer for success, but how they manage the results is another matter entirely. Miss Capricorn is conservative with her money and image, and wants to preserve what success has brought her. Mr. Leo is flamboyant, and wants to reward himself—and his friends—with the fruits of his labor. In work, and in relationships, they're both willing to take risks. Hers, however, are calculated, while his are spontaneous. In bed, it's easygoing. This bawdy woman surprises Mr. Leo by letting loose in this one area of her life. On a day-to-day basis, though, they have a lot to learn from one another. She could use a dash of his diva dramatics, while he could use a dose of her rationality. If they marry, they'll impress everyone with their achievements. However, the biggest achievements in this relationship will come about in their private life—when they've dropped their quest for fame and are just being themselves.

Leo Man & Aquarius Woman

Count Basie seeks Etta James.

Mr. Leo is astounded at how this woman observes the world without trying to make her own indelible mark on things. Sociable Miss Aquarius, always involved in other people's lives, defines herself through her dynamic clan of friends rather than through her own narrow ego. If anything, she likes to blend with her surroundings in order to better understand them. He takes the opposite approach. Mr. Leo likes to create drama wherever he goes, so nothing's happening anywhere until he shows up. She teaches him to look at the world as a place of many egos—not just his own—while he teaches her that sometimes making your own fun is better than watching others. Since they're both optimists, they can work the differences out, and make a long-lasting and funny couple.

Leo Man & Pisces Woman

Joe Jackson seeks Edie Brickell.

This sensitive, generous woman is the original do-gooder. She cares more about others than herself, a trait that Mr. Leo can't understand but that fascinates him. Beautiful, sensuous Miss Pisces doesn't do anything deliberate to attract attention to herself, and is content to let this overbearing man take center stage. She finds his egotism unnerving, but she appreciates his masculine bravado. She is often archetypally feminine and may like the way he takes care of her, allowing her to lose herself in artistic pursuits and saving the world. Ultimately, though, if they want to be together, Mr. Leo will have to tread more lightly around her feelings than he naturally does. He's comfortable with dramatic emotions, but doesn't know how to deal with her hurt silences. The drama between them is pronounced—especially in the bedroom—but they'll have to compromise to write a happy ending to their own love story.

Leo at Home

The Leo home is a spectacular showplace designed to impress a steady stream of guests. Homes owned by Lions are filled with oversized furniture, expensive art, and at least one giant fireplace. People born under this sign prefer an address that connotes wealth and class—from urban neighborhoods like Park Avenue and Beverly Hills to swanky outposts like Park City or Newport. Fire-ruled Leos love sun, so big windows and a porch are necessary. Where natural light doesn't brighten a room, they'll use lamps, mirrors, and candles set atop brass candlesticks to reflect their warm color scheme, which includes oranges, reds, deep golds, and shades of coral. The larger the Leo home, the better—this sign likes to have rooms to fit each mood, each with its own distinct style. The most spectacular room of all may be the bedroom, where Lions will have an opulent king-sized bed. Leos see this room as a shrine to their love life.

Leo Health

The Leo body is typically thin in youth, but expands in middle age. While folks born under this sign are rarely sedentary, since they dash from one engagement to the next, they tend to eat and snack a lot socially and can shun regular workouts. The Sun, which governs Leo, rules the heart, spine, and back, which means those born under this sign need to take back injuries seriously and also monitor their diet to guard against heart trouble. The Sun affects energy levels, which gives Leos a positive outlook but also means they need a lot of sleep. Leos don't enjoy exercise for its own sake, with the exception of dancing, which lets them express themselves. However, their vanity motivates them to maintain their good looks. Many people born under this sign try fad or quick weight-loss diets, as they like to see results right away. To really stay in shape, though, Leos need to create a regular exercise regimen that includes cardiovascular and toning work. To make the workout rewarding both physically and socially, Leos should join high-class gyms or hire a "personal trainer to the stars," reasoning that it hurts less if done in prestigious company.

Leo Style

Male and female Leos love couture clothes. Their wardrobe is one of the many canvases they use for self-expression, so staying ahead of the fashion curve is a priority to them. Leos like a deep, bright gold throughout their wardrobe—a color that gets others' attention, is warm, and reflects a Leo's bright personality. When it comes to jewelry, both male and female Lions opt for sparkling rubies. Shopping with a Leo is a treat. These folks skimp on nothing, and only go to stores where the service and tailoring are exquisite. In fact, they dress up to go shopping. Leos love scouring fashion magazines and inventing new ways to wear the season's designs. They also love to wear animal prints, suede, and anything in leather. Leos of both sexes wear designer everything—glasses, underwear, watches, and shoes. Even Leos who choose a sporty or antique look will wear designer sneakers or only the finest-quality vintage clothes. Coco Chanel, Gianfranco Ferre, Yves St. Laurent, and Anne Klein are among the designers born under this sign—folks whose creative looks suggest that the person who wears them has class and importance.

On the Road with Leo

Travel presents a conflict for Leos. On the one hand, these folks want to visit exotic, faraway places, but on the other, they just want to relax. Whichever they choose, bringing a lover and reserving a romantic place to stay will be at the top of their vacation list. Leos prefer luxury to budget travel and need their share of sunshine and pampering. A tour of the Mediterranean, a romantic villa in Tuscany, or a luxury resort in Cannes all appeal to the Leo's sensibilities. These folks also like to hit the "in" spots during high season, so they can be seen in Napa Valley during summer, the slopes of Chamonix each winter, or at the Thanksgiving Parade in New York each fall. Because Lions like night life, they may primp and preen on the beach during the day to rest up for a night of drama. They also love to bring home quality souvenirs—distinctive imported specialties that they can incorporate into their home or wardrobe and that double as conversation pieces.

Leo Entertaining

Leos treat every meal like a special occasion. Whether they're entertaining one friend or a party of ten, they like to create elaborate dishes and present them with a flourish. Their dining areas are typically decorated in warm golden colors and lit by a prominent chandelier or candles. Leo hosts pay attention to presentation and enjoy fanciful details—exotic appetizers before the meal, switching wines between courses, setting out finger bowls, or serving complicated dishes. They buy only the finest ingredients and bake with designer cookware. The dishes they serve will come straight from master chefs' cookbooks or a high-class catering company. Menus served by Leos typically include spicy, smoky flavors or grilled meats prepared with garlic and savory herbs. Spanish, Mexican, Thai, and Vietnamese cooking all appeal to the Leo's adventurous palate. These entertainers like to spoil guests and may overdo it with the number of courses they prepare. Guests always enjoy dinner with a Leo—even if they gain a few pounds.

In the Company of Leo

Musicians:
Tori Amos
Ian Anderson (Jethro Tull)
Patti Austin
Count Basie
Tony Bennett
Kate Bush
Belinda Carlisle (Go-Gos)
Benny Carter
Chuck D
Coolio
LL Cool J
Robert Cray
Dan Fogelberg
Jerry Garcia
  (Grateful Dead)
Gerri Halliwell
  (former Spice Girl)
Juliana Hatfield
Isaac Hayes
Buddy Holly
Whitney Houston
Joe Jackson
Mick Jagger
  (Rolling Stones)
Madonna
Aimee Mann
  ('Til Tuesday)
MCA (Beastie Boys)
Maureen McGovern
Robert Plant
  (Led Zeppelin)
Connie Stevens

Performers:
Ben Affleck
Gracie Allen
Gillian Anderson
Lucille Ball
Antonio Banderas
Halle Berry
Delta Burke
Julia Child
Connie Chung
Robert De Niro
David Duchovny
Hugh Grant
Woody Harrelson
Dustin Hoffman
Philip Seymour Hoffman
Gene Kelly
Lisa Kudrow
Myrna Loy
Steve Martin
Edward Norton
Sean Penn
Matthew Perry
Robert Redford
Arnold Schwarzenegger
Wesley Snipes
Kevin Spacey
Hillary Swank
Mae West

Reformers:
Bella Abzug
Napoleon Bonaparte
Fidel Castro
Bill Clinton
Davy Crockett
Amelia Earhart
Henry Ford
Harry F. Guggenheim
Dag Hammarskjöld
Herbert Hoover
Carl Jung
Jacqueline Kennedy Onassis

Artists:
Marcel Duchamp
Jenny Holzer
Grandma Moses
Maxfield Parrish
Paul Taylor
Andy Warhol

Athletes:
Kobe Bryant
Wilt Chamberlain
Peggy Fleming
Dorothy Hamill
Hulk Hogan
Magic Johnson
Karl Malone
Walter Payton
Pete Sampras

Writers:
Conrad Aiken
Isabel Allende
Russell Baker
James Baldwin
Wendell Berry
Ray Bradbury
Emily Brontë
Charles Bukowski
Caleb Carr
Raymond Chandler
Robertson Davies
Alexander Dumas
Edna Ferber
Mavis Gallant
O. Henry
Gerard Manley Hopkins
Ted Hughes
Aldous Huxley
Garrison Keillor
Herman Melville
Bharati Mukherjee
V. S. Naipaul
Dorothy Parker
Beatrix Potter
E. Annie Proulx
Percy Bysshe Shelley
Danielle Steel
Jacqueline Susann
Booth Tarkington
Alfred Lord Tennyson
Leon Uris

Permissions

Everybody Wants to Rule the World
Tears for Fears
(Roland Orzabal/Ian Stanley/Manny Elias)
℗ 1985 Phonogram Ltd. (London), courtesy of Universal Music Enterprises, a Division of UMG Recordings, Inc.

I'm the Man
Joe Jackson
(Joe Jackson)
℗ 1979 A&M Records, Inc., courtesy of Universal Music Enterprises, a Division of UMG Recordings, Inc.

Wonderful World, Beautiful People
Jimmy Cliff
(Jimmy Cliff)
℗ 1969 Trojan Records Ltd., courtesy of Trojan Records Ltd.

Firecracker
Mass Production
(Ricardo Williams)
℗ 1979 Atlantic Recording Corp., produced under license from Atlantic Recording Corp.

Accentuate the Positive
Dr. John
(Harold Arlen/Johnny Mercer)
℗ 1989 Warner Bros. Records, Inc., produced under license from Warner Bros. Records, Inc.

Leader of the Pack
The Shangri-Las
(Jeff Barry/Ellie Greenwich/George Morton)
Courtesy of Universal Music Enterprises, a Division of UMG Recordings, Inc.

Leo Rising
Ronnie Montrose
(Ronnie Montrose)
℗ 1978 Warner Bros. Records, Inc., produced under license from Warner Bros. Records Inc.

A Beautiful Morning
The Rascals
(Eddie Brigati/Felix Cavaliere)
Produced under license from Atlantic Recording Corp.

You Make Me Feel Like Dancing
Leo Sayer
(Leo Sayer/Vini Poncia)
℗ 1976 Warner Bros. Records, Inc., produced under license from Warner Bros. Records Inc.

Drama Queen
Belloluna
(John C. Brand)
℗ 1997 Sidereal Music, courtesy of Daemon Records.

Save the Last Dance for Me
The Drifters
(Doc Pomus/Mort Shuman)
Produced under license from Atlantic Recording Corp.

Leo
Cannonball Adderley featuring The Nat Adderley Sextet
(Nat Adderley/Rick Holmes)
℗ 1972 Capitol Records, Inc., under license from EMI-Capitol Music Special Markets.

This Compilation ℗ 2001 Rhino Entertainment Company.